Complete Hor

Virgo 2023

Monthly astrological forecasts for 2023

TATIANA BORSCH

Translated from Russian by Sonja Swenson
Translation copyright © Coinflow Limited, Cyprus
AstraArt Books is an imprint of Coinflow limited, Cyprus
Published by Coinflow Limited, Cyprus
For queries please contact: tatianaborsch@yahoo.com

ISBN978-9925-609-17-8(paperback)
ISBN 978-9925-609-18-5(ebook)

Contents

2023 –The Great Transition Continues

In previous forecasts, I have described the unique transition period in which the world finds itself.

I will summarize for those who have not read my predictions for 2020, 2021, and 2022.

We have entered a period of changes, and the world has come to a fateful point, where everything that seemed constant and unshakable no longer is. If that is the case, then what awaits us?

From an astrological perspective, 2020, 2021, and 2022 are extensions of one long period, and cannot be divided. This is a time of major changes in every nation, home, and individual.

There is no comparison for this period in modern history. In fact, humanity has not lived through a period quite like this for a very long time.

The astrological explanation for this is that we are living through a grandiose shift in eras. The Age of Pisces, which lasted for 2,160 years, is transitioning into the Age of Aquarius.

2023 fits naturally into this complex sequence. This is an important and critical watershed.

During the first half of 2023, we see a natural continuation of a very complicated period that began in 2022. The confrontation between East and West will continue in Ukraine, as will rivalry between the United States and China, along with financial and economic crises that have beset the entire world.

As of June 2022, when this forecast is being written, I can predict that in the fall of 2022, that is in October and November, the conflict between Russia and the West in Ukraine will reach a new level. Russia's advancements will force the West, including the United States, to take on a more active role in the face of the invasion in Ukraine, as the entire world risks being dragged into a new war.

The stars predict that the war in Ukraine may come to an end in January-February 2023. Ukraine will be divided into two zones of influence, with much of its territory falling under Russia's shadow. Volodymyr Zelenskyy will lose his grip on power and may flee the country, and Ukrainian leadership will be replaced. Peace initiatives that might otherwise be capable of changing this tragic situation will constantly be thwarted. In January 2023, aggressive Mars will no longer be in retrograde, and by February, there will be a light at the end of the tunnel. Initially, it will be just a flicker, but it is certainly better than nothing.

Gradually, the countries involved in this conflict will come to realize that they need to hold constructive negotiations in order to meet all of society's healthy demands and trends. These talks will not be swift, and they will probably only bear fruit in the second half of 2023.

Overall, despite Ukraine's valiant efforts both militarily and politically, along with support from the West, Russia will prevail, militarily, geopolitically, and ideologically.

This will seriously alter the geopolitical landscape on the global stage. In time, Asia and Russia will dominate the world's economy. The events of this year are just one more step in the transition as global influence shifts eastward. Tensions between the United States and Asian countries will only heat up.

In late 2022 and early 2023, many countries' economies will descend into chaos, and a general financial crisis will drag down banks, companies, and the entire planet's population.

In many Western countries, antiwar sentiment will be palpable, and there may be demonstrations, protests, and other expressions of dissatisfaction with governments.

In Russia, the fall of 2022 and first half of 2023 will see widespread changes in the structures of power. Western sanctions will lead to serious economic losses, forcing Russia to find a way to survive in the face of Western and American economic aggression.

The worst economic crisis will take place in the United States. The fall of 2022 and during the first half of 2023 may be the worst period it has faced in recent memory. There may be serious confrontations between political parties, which might throw American society as a whole off balance. During the fall of 2022 and first half of 2023, President Biden will experience serious difficulties. The stars predict he will face worsening health, along with serious destabilization of the entire American financial system. (A president's horoscope is responsible for much of what will happen to his or her country). During the same period, Bident's great foe, former President Trump, is expected to become much more active and powerful.

European countries will not be spared, either. In France, opposition to President Macron's policies will grow and Macron will lose some of his influence.

In Germany, Chancellor Olaf Scholz will become more aggressive during the fall. Despite his outward calm, he may turn out to be an active supporter of Western support for Ukraine. This will lead to a backlash in German society, and by May 2023, Scholz will be in a much weaker position than he is today.

From November 2022 to May 2023, the United Kingdom may see changes in leadership. This will be a period full of obstacles, including serious financial difficulties, demonstrations by those who disagree with the political power structure, and a trend of separatism in the various regions. In June-July, things will calm down significantly, and the British financial and political system will manage to recover.

The second half of May will also be a time of challenges. Jupiter will square Pluto during this time, with support from aggressive Mars. We can expect cataclysms and changes in many countries' governments here. Serious acts of terrorism cannot be ruled out, either.

During the second half of 2023, Jupiter will transition from the bellicose sign of Aries into the more peaceful sign of Taurus, and its favorable aspect with Saturn in June gives reason to hope that things are likely to improve.

That process will not be overnight, however. We see evidence of that in Uranus, which will be in the sign of Taurus, at the same degrees as during the period of World War II. Taurus symbolizes life and all its peaceful manifestations, while Uranus is the symbol of renewal through destruction. That portends a break with old structures, which may unleash war, death, and political and economic clashes.

All of these painful processes will eventually lead to the birth of a new, modern world, but that will not be completed until after 2025.

Looking at the future, I predict that in late 2022, and early 2023, economic, political, and social, as well as personal crises will reach a peak. Remember, we are blessed to live in an era of great change, and historical events certainly do leave their mark on our personal lives.

I also predict that during the second half of 2023, we will reach the halfway point on this long and winding road, and this may be the most complicated part of that trajectory. After this point, people will begin looking for a way to resolve the world's most pressing problems, and the light at the end of the tunnel may start to glimmer a bit brighter. Of course, this is inevitable, but step by step, people will start to tackle the many challenges we face. This is a gradual, sometimes painful process. But there is hope that Fate will have less unpleasant surprises in store for us and life will start running a bit more smoothly. It will never go back to exactly the way it was, but as this period draws to a close, we will see that in one way or another, all of these changes are for the best.

Money

We may face a global banking system crisis, which is likely to happen in November-December 2022. I believe it would be wiser to hold your money in something tangible, like real estate, land, or gold, than in the banking system or simply on paper. Purchasing power may experience a serious decline.

Health

Health-wise, anyone with thyroid problems or cardiovascular disease or any illnesses involving the blood vessels of the brain should be particularly cautious. We see this as Uranus transits into Taurus.

Pluto is still in Capricorn, which exacerbates musculoskeletal and bone disorders. Teeth are also in Pluto's crosshairs, so it is best to treat them quickly!

Cancer cases may rise, so do not hesitate to visit the doctor quickly, as cancer is only treatable in the early stages.

In 2023, Saturn is transiting into Pisces – this may lead to problems for those with various types of diabetes or problems involving the legs.

During the spring and fall of 2023, more outbreaks of unknown diseases and viruses are possible.

Nature

In 2023, various natural anomalies that the world has been struggling with may continue. Jupiter in Aries might cause fires, which will be a destabilizing factor during the winter and spring of 2023.

However, in early May, when Jupiter transitions into Taurus, we can expect to see significant improvements in agriculture. Harvests will be more abundant, which, in many countries, will mean a way out of the food crisis. Many countries will also be able to invest more in agriculture production and processing, which will only revive small towns and villages.

Fashion

Jupiter will be in Aries during the first half of 2023, and this promises all shades of red, which will be on models everywhere during this period. Many people will instinctively be drawn to red, as Aries's energy simply hangs in the air. Military-inspired dress may also be on the runways.

During the second half of 2023, Jupiter will transition into Taurus, which is primarily green in color. This is a great color, as it symbolizes growth and rebirth. Taurus's second color is pink, which symbolizes romanticism, softness, love for sensual pleasures and enjoyment. The fashion world may respond in kind with light, floaty fabrics and perhaps a new focus on femininity.

Have a wonderful year! Don't be afraid of crises, as they bring with them new opportunities!

Always,

Tatiana Borsch

2023 Overview for Virgo

Hold on! You are embarking on a turbulent year in all areas of your life. This might be beneficial to you, as you have to crack a few eggs to make an omelet.

Work. This year, you might have to understand that the time has come to begin a new chapter in your professional life. Both business owners and employees can expect major changes. In many cases, that will involve overhauling your entire lifestyle – expect a move to a new city or even abroad.

Alternatively, you may be totally renewing your business or taking on new responsibilities with a new organization. You will not feel these changes until May or June, and the first part of the year may still feel somewhat confusing and involve difficult organizational tasks to prepare for the changes underway.

From May to October, you will be very busy, and that is generally a very good thing. But by the fall, many of your achievements will be in doubt once again.

In some cases, this may involve auditing bodies, or possibly business partners from afar or foreign laws.

You will manage to get a handle on this all quickly, and by the holidays, most of your problems will be resolved in your favor.

Money. Financially, the first half of the year is difficult and will be until May. February may be the bright spot here, when you are highly likely to receive a large sum of money.

During the second half of the year, things are looking much more optimistic, especially in May, June, and late September and October.

Love and family. Slowly but surely, you are feeling alienated in your personal life, as things cool off with your spouse or long-term partner, if you have had problems in the past.

Severe Saturn, which has been in the sector of the sky responsible for relationships for some time, is demanding you answer for your past mistakes. If there are not many of them, you will be alright, but if you have a trail of guilt behind you, take a long, hard look at your behavior and reassess. Otherwise, you might expect a separation.

In families that get along, you might be working on home improvements, and the first half of the year will be particularly telling, when you may see major repairs or perhaps even buy new real estate.

In some cases, you will move to another city or abroad. Those planning this major undertaking can count on something happening in the spring or summer of 2023.

Over the fall, you will face some obstacles, as moving abroad involves dealing with foreign laws and other challenges.

Alternatively, you might face someone hostile in your circle, which you will feel the most in October or November.

In the fall of 2023, you might have to grapple with various problems involving relatives. Expect a quarrel with a family member, and November may be the most difficult time for this.

Health. When it comes to your health, the most difficult time is from January to April. Here, you need to take care of yourself and remember that health comes first, and the rest will follow. Be very careful if you are weakened or elderly – at the first sign of illness, don't try to be your own doctor and instead turn to a professional.

During the same period, you may feel fatigued even if you are otherwise healthy. Women should see a cosmetologist more often or at least take better care of themselves at home.

After May, things will improve. Jupiter will transition to a friendly sign, which will be reflected in all areas of your life, including your mood and self-esteem.

In October and November, be more careful when driving and traveling.

January

New York Time			London Time		
Calendar Day	Lunar Day	Lunar Day Start Time	Calendar Day	Lunar Day	Lunar Day Start Time
01/01/2023	11	12:58 PM	01/01/2023	10	12:31 PM
02/01/2023	12	1:32 PM	02/01/2023	11	12:56 PM
03/01/2023	13	2:10 PM	03/01/2023	12	1:27 PM
04/01/2023	14	2:53 PM	04/01/2023	13	2:05 PM
05/01/2023	15	3:42 PM	05/01/2023	14	2:51 PM
06/01/2023	16	4:36 PM	06/01/2023	15	3:45 PM
07/01/2023	17	5:32 PM	07/01/2023	16	4:45 PM
08/01/2023	18	6:31 PM	08/01/2023	17	5:50 PM
09/01/2023	19	7:30 PM	09/01/2023	18	6:56 PM
10/01/2023	20	8:29 PM	10/01/2023	19	8:04 PM
11/01/2023	21	9:28 PM	11/01/2023	20	9:11 PM
12/01/2023	22	10:28 PM	12/01/2023	21	10:19 PM
13/01/2023	23	11:29 PM	13/01/2023	22	11:28 PM
15/01/2023	24	12:32 AM	15/01/2023	23	12:40 AM
16/01/2023	25	1:38 AM	16/01/2023	24	1:54 AM
17/01/2023	26	2:47 AM	17/01/2023	25	3:11 AM
18/01/2023	27	3:56 AM	18/01/2023	26	4:28 AM
19/01/2023	28	5:05 AM	19/01/2023	27	5:42 AM
20/01/2023	29	6:08 AM	20/01/2023	28	6:46 AM
21/01/2023	30	7:02 AM	21/01/2023	29	7:38 AM
21/01/2023	1	3:55 PM	21/01/2023	1	8:55 PM
22/01/2023	2	7:49 AM	22/01/2023	2	8:17 AM
23/01/2023	3	8:28 AM	23/01/2023	3	8:48 AM
24/01/2023	4	9:01 AM	24/01/2023	4	9:13 AM
25/01/2023	5	9:32 AM	25/01/2023	5	9:34 AM
26/01/2023	6	10:01 AM	26/01/2023	6	9:54 AM
27/01/2023	7	10:30 AM	27/01/2023	7	10:14 AM
28/01/2023	8	11:00 AM	28/01/2023	8	10:35 AM
29/01/2023	9	11:33 AM	29/01/2023	9	11:00 AM
30/01/2023	10	12:10 PM	30/01/2023	10	11:29 AM
31/01/2023	11	12:52 PM	31/01/2023	11	12:04 PM

You can find the description of each lunar day in the chapter "A Guide to The Moon Cycle and Lunar Days"

In January, your greatest task is to do the right thing and help those in need – and you can! The idea that nice guys never win could not be further from the truth!

Work. The first 20 days of January are likely to look rather gloomy at work. First of all, everyone is sluggish coming back from the holidays, and secondly, Mercury, your ruler, will be in retrograde until January 19, while Mars will be in retrograde until the 12th.

That means that any major changes in the workplace that you began in the second half of 2022 are still underway, and you will be able to safely deal with it all during the last 10 days of the month. If you run into any resistance from management or disagreements with your partners, everything will fall into place closer to the end of the month.

Entrepreneurs and managers at every level will face the difficult task of renewing their business.

Employees might leave their current job to look for something new. The last 10 days of the month are best for this endeavor, or all of February. It is highly likely that you will have to continue working where you are for some time, but that is temporary. Keep that in mind as you seek out greener grasses.

Money. The first 20 days of January are ruinous for you, financially speaking. You will be pouring money into your home and professional goals. However, Virgos will be able to count on a welcome surprise – a gift from a loved one, or perhaps a small prize.

The last 10 days of the month are looking more stable and prosperous. Everything will return to normal, and you can expect the greatest sums of money on January 30 and 31.

Love and family. The first 20 days of January are likely to find Virgos busy with children and loved ones. You might take a trip or meet with relatives and old friends.

The stars strongly advise you to pay close attention to your relationship with your spouse or partner. Jupiter, the planet of good fortune that has been propping up your marriage sector, is moving to another sign, and you will have to deal with any challenges on your own. Remember that when it comes to love, the less you demand, the more you get, and act accordingly.

Health. January sees you bounding with energy, and you have no reason to fear falling ill. It is a good time for any trips to the spa or various minor cosmetic procedures but avoid the first 20 days of the month for any plastic surgeries or major procedures, as Mercury and Mars will both be in retrograde.

February

New York Time			London Time		
Calendar Day	Lunar Day	Lunar Day Start Time	Calendar Day	Lunar Day	Lunar Day Start Time
01/02/2023	12	1:38 PM	01/02/2023	12	12:48 PM
02/02/2023	13	2:30 PM	02/02/2023	13	1:39 PM
03/02/2023	14	3:26 PM	03/02/2023	14	2:37 PM
04/02/2023	15	4:24 PM	04/02/2023	15	3:41 PM
05/02/2023	16	5:23 PM	05/02/2023	16	4:47 PM
06/02/2023	17	6:22 PM	06/02/2023	17	5:54 PM
07/02/2023	18	7:22 PM	07/02/2023	18	7:02 PM
08/02/2023	19	8:22 PM	08/02/2023	19	8:10 PM
09/02/2023	20	9:22 PM	09/02/2023	20	9:19 PM
10/02/2023	21	10:24 PM	10/02/2023	21	10:28 PM
11/02/2023	22	11:27 PM	11/02/2023	22	11:40 PM
13/02/2023	23	12:33 AM	13/02/2023	23	12:54 AM
14/02/2023	24	1:40 AM	14/02/2023	24	2:09 AM
15/02/2023	25	2:46 AM	15/02/2023	25	3:22 AM
16/02/2023	26	3:50 AM	16/02/2023	26	4:28 AM
17/02/2023	27	4:47 AM	17/02/2023	27	5:24 AM
18/02/2023	28	5:36 AM	18/02/2023	28	6:09 AM
19/02/2023	29	6:19 AM	19/02/2023	29	6:44 AM
20/02/2023	1	2:09 AM	20/02/2023	1	7:09 AM
20/02/2023	2	6:55 AM	20/02/2023	2	7:11 AM
21/02/2023	3	7:28 AM	21/02/2023	3	7:35 AM
22/02/2023	4	7:58 AM	22/02/2023	4	7:56 AM
23/02/2023	5	8:28 AM	23/02/2023	5	8:16 AM
24/02/2023	6	8:59 AM	24/02/2023	6	8:38 AM
25/02/2023	7	9:32 AM	25/02/2023	7	9:02 AM
26/02/2023	8	10:08 AM	26/02/2023	8	9:30 AM
27/02/2023	9	10:49 AM	27/02/2023	9	10:03 AM
28/02/2023	10	11:34 AM	28/02/2023	10	10:44 AM

You can find the description of each lunar day in the chapter "A Guide to The Moon Cycle and Lunar Days"

The changes continue, both at work and at home, though your life is looking much more calm, predictable, and like something you can handle. The chaos you felt before is now a thing of the past.

Work. February moves quickly, and you will be busy and productive. Business owners and managers of every level are likely to be preparing for some changes in their business. Everything you do in February will have a major impact on your professional status and become the cornerstone of your future success.

Real estate transactions will turn out in your favor, and that is directly related to expanding or reorienting your business.

In some cases, you may be planning to expand to other cities or abroad.

Employees will find that their employers are restructuring this month. In some cases, they will remain where they are, while in others, they may soon find themselves seeking a better place for their talents, and it is worth taking that into consideration this month.

Despite the positive and relatively productive atmosphere in February, during the first 10 days of the month, you may run into some obstacles. That may be due to business partners in other cities or abroad, or possibly involve resolving legal disputes. In either case, however, the quandary is sure to be resolved in your favor.

Money. In February, your finances are looking strong. You will have a steady income, and noticeably more of it. Expect the largest sums to come in on February 1, 10, 11, 18, 27, and 28. Your expenses are low, reasonable, and predictable.

Love and family. In your personal life, your partner will take initiative this month. If he or she suggests moving to a new home, apartment, or abroad, so be it. Real estate transactions will be at the top of many families' agendas.

The first 10 days of the month are likely to present some challenges for you emotionally. During this time, spouses may have opposing views of various domestic issues, and experience differing moods, as well. Things will get complicated if you have a history of misunderstandings or shared business.

In other cases, you may be grappling with jealousy or different demands of one another. Expect some knock-down, drag-out fights during the first 10 days of the month, which will then fade into nothing.

The situation is similar for unmarried couples.

Children are a source of happiness, and they are experiencing positive changes in their own lives. Many families will be expecting new children or grandchildren.

Health. In February, you are feeling a bit tired, but this will not cause any serious trouble, as long as you lead an exceedingly healthy lifestyle and take utmost care of yourself. February is a great time to quit any bad habits or undergo any wellness procedures.

March

New York Time			London Time		
Calendar Day	Lunar Day	Lunar Day Start Time	Calendar Day	Lunar Day	Lunar Day Start Time
01/03/2023	11	12:24 PM	01/03/2023	11	11:33 AM
02/03/2023	12	1:19 PM	02/03/2023	12	12:29 PM
03/03/2023	13	2:16 PM	03/03/2023	13	1:31 PM
04/03/2023	14	3:15 PM	04/03/2023	14	2:36 PM
05/03/2023	15	4:15 PM	05/03/2023	15	3:44 PM
06/03/2023	16	5:14 PM	06/03/2023	16	4:52 PM
07/03/2023	17	6:15 PM	07/03/2023	17	6:00 PM
08/03/2023	18	7:15 PM	08/03/2023	18	7:09 PM
09/03/2023	19	8:17 PM	09/03/2023	19	8:19 PM
10/03/2023	20	9:20 PM	10/03/2023	20	9:31 PM
11/03/2023	21	10:25 PM	11/03/2023	21	10:44 PM
13/03/2023	22	12:31 AM	12/03/2023	22	11:58 PM
14/03/2023	23	1:37 AM	14/03/2023	23	1:11 AM
15/03/2023	24	2:40 AM	15/03/2023	24	2:18 AM
16/03/2023	25	3:37 AM	16/03/2023	25	3:16 AM
17/03/2023	26	4:28 AM	17/03/2023	26	4:03 AM
18/03/2023	27	5:12 AM	18/03/2023	27	4:41 AM
19/03/2023	28	5:50 AM	19/03/2023	28	5:10 AM
20/03/2023	29	6:23 AM	20/03/2023	29	5:35 AM
21/03/2023	30	6:54 AM	21/03/2023	30	5:57 AM
21/03/2023	1	1:26 PM	21/03/2023	1	5:26 PM
22/03/2023	2	7:24 AM	22/03/2023	2	6:17 AM
23/03/2023	3	7:55 AM	23/03/2023	3	6:38 AM
24/03/2023	4	8:27 AM	24/03/2023	4	7:01 AM
25/03/2023	5	9:03 AM	25/03/2023	5	7:28 AM
26/03/2023	6	9:43 AM	26/03/2023	6	9:00 AM
27/03/2023	7	10:27 AM	27/03/2023	7	9:38 AM
28/03/2023	8	11:16 AM	28/03/2023	8	10:25 AM
29/03/2023	9	12:10 PM	29/03/2023	9	11:19 AM
30/03/2023	10	1:07 PM	30/03/2023	10	12:19 PM
31/03/2023	11	2:05 PM	31/03/2023	11	1:24 PM

You can find the description of each lunar day in the chapter "A Guide to The Moon Cycle and Lunar Days"

This month, you are still between a rock and a hard place. The ball is in other people's court. Be a team player if you can, and if you can't, wait for an opportunity to move forward on your own.

Work. You are looking down a month full of meetings and active networking. You will be busy negotiating with partners, and the topic at hand may be future business development or financial in nature.

Business owners and managers at every level might be striving to expand their business and seek out new resources for this endeavor.

Your efforts will pan out – during the first and last 10 days of the month, you can count on constructive negotiations and a nice amount of money.

During the second 10 days of March, you may run into minor disagreements with partners about your business organization, but by the last 10 days, this will be a thing of the past.

Employees are likely to encounter disagreements with management, competitors, and problems on their team during the second 10 days of March. The stars recommend avoiding any open confrontation. The results will be better if you tread lightly and remain diplomatic.

The most important events in March will be related to colleagues from other cities or abroad – you might be developing a lot of ideas with their direct participation and support.

Any travel planned for this month will be a success.

Money. March is a great time for your finances, but the money in question is unlikely to be yours. Rather, you can count on financial support from partners, beneficial loans, or successful credit transactions.

Those who are not part of the working world will receive financial support from a loved one, parents, or a spouse. You might also profit from a successful real estate transaction.

Love and family. Your personal life is very busy this month.

Couples who get along will be busy working on their home and with various real estate transactions. Many will be planning a move – perhaps to a new home, or, more extravagantly, to another city or even abroad. If this is the case, March is a great month to get ready for this massive undertaking. Your loved one will be able to manage a lot and take on a great deal.

Things will turn out somewhat differently for those who recently decided to separate or divorce. You will spend March deciding who owes whom what. The stars predict you will be pleased with the outcome.

Health. This month, you are feeling a bit under the weather, and those who are elderly or weakened should be particularly cautious. Take care of yourself and if you need to, see a specialist and avoid trying to be your own doctor.

April

New York Time			London Time		
Calendar Day	Lunar Day	Lunar Day Start Time	Calendar Day	Lunar Day	Lunar Day Start Time
01/04/2023	12	3:04 PM	01/04/2023	12	2:30 PM
02/04/2023	13	4:04 PM	02/04/2023	13	3:38 PM
03/04/2023	14	5:04 PM	03/04/2023	14	4:46 PM
04/04/2023	15	6:05 PM	04/04/2023	15	5:56 PM
05/04/2023	16	7:07 PM	05/04/2023	16	7:06 PM
06/04/2023	17	8:11 PM	06/04/2023	17	8:18 PM
07/04/2023	18	9:16 PM	07/04/2023	18	9:32 PM
08/04/2023	19	10:23 PM	08/04/2023	19	10:47 PM
09/04/2023	20	11:30 PM	10/04/2023	20	12:02 AM
11/04/2023	21	12:34 AM	11/04/2023	21	1:11 AM
12/04/2023	22	1:33 AM	12/04/2023	22	2:12 AM
13/04/2023	23	2:25 AM	13/04/2023	23	3:02 AM
14/04/2023	24	3:10 AM	14/04/2023	24	3:41 AM
15/04/2023	25	3:48 AM	15/04/2023	25	4:12 AM
16/04/2023	26	4:22 AM	16/04/2023	26	4:38 AM
17/04/2023	27	4:53 AM	17/04/2023	27	5:00 AM
18/04/2023	28	5:22 AM	18/04/2023	28	5:20 AM
19/04/2023	29	5:52 AM	19/04/2023	29	5:40 AM
20/04/2023	1	12:15 AM	20/04/2023	1	5:15 AM
20/04/2023	2	6:23 AM	20/04/2023	2	6:02 AM
21/04/2023	3	6:57 AM	21/04/2023	3	6:27 AM
22/04/2023	4	7:35 AM	22/04/2023	4	6:56 AM
23/04/2023	5	8:18 AM	23/04/2023	5	7:32 AM
24/04/2023	6	9:06 AM	24/04/2023	6	8:15 AM
25/04/2023	7	9:59 AM	25/04/2023	7	9:07 AM
26/04/2023	8	10:55 AM	26/04/2023	8	10:06 AM
27/04/2023	9	11:53 AM	27/04/2023	9	11:09 AM
28/04/2023	10	12:52 PM	28/04/2023	10	12:15 PM
29/04/2023	11	1:52 PM	29/04/2023	11	1:23 PM
30/04/2023	12	2:51 PM	30/04/2023	12	2:30 PM

You can find the description of each lunar day in the chapter "A Guide to The Moon Cycle and Lunar Days"

All month long, you are able to demonstrate your speed, discipline, and hard-working nature. These qualities, along with your detail-oriented ways, are sure to lead to incredible results. Go for it!

Work. Your main task this month is to convince your business partners of your amazing ideas and that they should make an investment. The stars predict that this is necessary if you want to develop your business. If you don't have reliable colleagues, it is worth focusing on finding some. April is a perfect time for this. You can expect new acquaintances, meetings, and negotiations in which you catch the eye of the people you need. Be bold as you strive for your goals, and it is reasonable to take on a bit of risk right now. Remember that a lot is riding on your ability to sell your ideas, so stock up on arguments and back them up with facts where you can. The stars are on your side.

Close to the end of the month, you will spend more time communicating with colleagues in other cities or abroad, and you might take a successful trip. Your ideas might interest a partner from afar.

Money. Despite your clear success when it comes to networking this month, things are not so smooth when it comes to money. But don't get too down about it – you will have money soon. Everything you do in April will pay off, perhaps not overnight, but in a little bit. You are unlikely to end up bankrupt in April, though you will probably have less to spend than you had planned on.

Love and family. There are a lot of changes in your personal life. Couples who get along are able to reach mutual understanding and agree with one another. Your loved one will be on a winning streak, which is reason for you to celebrate.

Those who recently separated or lost a loved one might count on a favorable resolution to your material problems this month, as well as a new person in your life.

You have been waiting for stability in your relationship, and now, the time has come, and this goes for all Virgos, whether you are married, in a long-term relationship, or just beginning a new romance.

Closer to the end of the month or maybe in May, you can expect to go on a trip, and it will be a great success.

Health. In April, you are not feeling as energetic as usual, and that will be most noticeable during the New Moon on April 1 and 2, as well as the Full Moon on April 15-17. During these times, try to take care of yourself and take whatever measures you must.

May

New York Time			London Time		
Calendar Day	Lunar Day	Lunar Day Start Time	Calendar Day	Lunar Day	Lunar Day Start Time
01/05/2023	13	3:52 PM	01/05/2023	13	3:39 PM
02/05/2023	14	4:53 PM	02/05/2023	14	4:48 PM
03/05/2023	15	5:56 PM	03/05/2023	15	6:00 PM
04/05/2023	16	7:02 PM	04/05/2023	16	7:14 PM
05/05/2023	17	8:09 PM	05/05/2023	17	8:30 PM
06/05/2023	18	9:18 PM	06/05/2023	18	9:47 PM
07/05/2023	19	10:25 PM	07/05/2023	19	11:00 PM
08/05/2023	20	11:27 PM	09/05/2023	20	12:06 AM
10/05/2023	21	12:22 AM	10/05/2023	21	1:01 AM
11/05/2023	22	1:10 AM	11/05/2023	22	1:43 AM
12/05/2023	23	1:50 AM	12/05/2023	23	2:16 AM
13/05/2023	24	2:24 AM	13/05/2023	24	2:43 AM
14/05/2023	25	2:55 AM	14/05/2023	25	3:05 AM
15/05/2023	26	3:24 AM	15/05/2023	26	3:25 AM
16/05/2023	27	3:53 AM	16/05/2023	27	3:45 AM
17/05/2023	28	4:23 AM	17/05/2023	28	4:05 AM
18/05/2023	29	4:55 AM	18/05/2023	29	4:28 AM
19/05/2023	30	5:31 AM	19/05/2023	30	4:55 AM
19/05/2023	1	11:55 AM	19/05/2023	1	4:55 PM
20/05/2023	2	6:11 AM	20/05/2023	2	5:27 AM
21/05/2023	3	6:57 AM	21/05/2023	3	6:08 AM
22/05/2023	4	7:48 AM	22/05/2023	4	6:56 AM
23/05/2023	5	8:44 AM	23/05/2023	5	7:53 AM
24/05/2023	6	9:42 AM	24/05/2023	6	8:55 AM
25/05/2023	7	10:41 AM	25/05/2023	7	10:01 AM
26/05/2023	8	11:40 AM	26/05/2023	8	11:07 AM
27/05/2023	9	12:39 PM	27/05/2023	9	12:14 PM
28/05/2023	10	1:38 PM	28/05/2023	10	1:22 PM
29/05/2023	11	2:38 PM	29/05/2023	11	2:30 PM
30/05/2023	12	3:39 PM	30/05/2023	12	3:40 PM
31/05/2023	13	4:43 PM	31/05/2023	13	4:52 PM

You can find the description of each lunar day in the chapter "A Guide to The Moon Cycle and Lunar Days"

This month, your path in life seems long and winding. Your strategic task is to come up with a clear plan of action and slowly begin moving in your chosen direction. Don't expect anything to be fast, right now.

Work. This month, many Virgos will have a run-in with an unfortunate mishap at work. Your ruler, Mercury, is in retrograde, and in your case, that means red tape, the people you need suddenly disappearing, and issues involving auditing agencies.

Those with ties to colleagues in other cities or abroad will also face hardships. You may spend a long time hashing out future cooperation, making adjustments, and thinking up projects.

Most of the difficulties will appear during the first 20 days of the month. The last 10 days will be more positive – you be able to make a decisive step forward into the future.

Money. Financially, May brings a lot of ups and downs. It's not that the money won't be there, but your expenses will be rather extreme. That may involve work, or perhaps your family.

Love and family. Things are not easy in your personal life, either. You have felt warm feelings for someone for some time now, but things are suddenly cooling off. That distance is dangerous, as it may lead to a separation.

Spouses are also on a slippery path of misunderstandings and quarrels, and it is worth understanding that there are troubled waters ahead, and your relationship will require sincerity, warmth, and attention. "Happy wife, happy life" might just be the guidance you need, right now.

Partners who get along might work together to tackle issues related to housing and real estate, which will move closer to a logical conclusion.

Any trips planned in May will turn out well, but the stars recommend sticking to places you have been to before.

Health. This month, you are not feeling particularly energetic, so take care of yourself and don't try to test your body with any excess.

June

New York Time			London Time		
Calendar Day	Lunar Day	Lunar Day Start Time	Calendar Day	Lunar Day	Lunar Day Start Time
01/06/2023	14	5:50 PM	01/06/2023	14	6:07 PM
02/06/2023	15	6:59 PM	02/06/2023	15	7:24 PM
03/06/2023	16	8:08 PM	03/06/2023	16	8:41 PM
04/06/2023	17	9:14 PM	04/06/2023	17	9:52 PM
05/06/2023	18	10:14 PM	05/06/2023	18	10:53 PM
06/06/2023	19	11:06 PM	06/06/2023	19	11:41 PM
07/06/2023	20	11:50 PM	08/06/2023	20	12:19 AM
09/06/2023	21	12:27 AM	09/06/2023	21	12:48 AM
10/06/2023	22	12:59 AM	10/06/2023	22	1:11 AM
11/06/2023	23	1:29 AM	11/06/2023	23	1:32 AM
12/06/2023	24	1:57 AM	12/06/2023	24	1:52 AM
13/06/2023	25	2:26 AM	13/06/2023	25	2:11 AM
14/06/2023	26	2:56 AM	14/06/2023	26	2:33 AM
15/06/2023	27	3:30 AM	15/06/2023	27	2:57 AM
16/06/2023	28	4:08 AM	16/06/2023	28	3:27 AM
17/06/2023	29	4:51 AM	17/06/2023	29	4:04 AM
18/06/2023	1	12:39 AM	18/06/2023	30	4:49 AM
18/06/2023	2	5:40 AM	18/06/2023	1	5:39 AM
19/06/2023	3	6:34 AM	19/06/2023	2	5:42 AM
20/06/2023	4	7:31 AM	20/06/2023	3	6:43 AM
21/06/2023	5	8:30 AM	21/06/2023	4	7:47 AM
22/06/2023	6	9:29 AM	22/06/2023	5	8:54 AM
23/06/2023	7	10:28 AM	23/06/2023	6	10:01 AM
24/06/2023	8	11:27 AM	24/06/2023	7	11:07 AM
25/06/2023	9	12:25 PM	25/06/2023	8	12:14 PM
26/06/2023	10	1:25 PM	26/06/2023	9	1:22 PM
27/06/2023	11	2:27 PM	27/06/2023	10	2:32 PM
28/06/2023	12	3:31 PM	28/06/2023	11	3:44 PM
29/06/2023	13	4:37 PM	29/06/2023	12	4:59 PM
30/06/2023	14	5:46 PM	30/06/2023	13	6:15 PM

You can find the description of each lunar day in the chapter "A Guide to The Moon Cycle and Lunar Days"

You are embarking on a period for which you have been preparing for some time. The time for talking is over, now, it's time to act!

Work. June is an incredibly important month for your career. You will be able to confirm your longstanding ideas and ambitious plans.

You might renew contact with old business partners, some of whom may live in other cities or abroad. You are beginning a new period in your career, and maybe your life, which will change literally everything. You may be making important steps in this direction already in June, or maybe it will come later in 2023.

You may be making plans related to a move, opening a business in another city or abroad. Alternatively, you may spend a lot of time traveling for work.

Employees will be negotiating a new job, and this will be very successful. You may already be starting your new job this month, and your old friends will be there to lend a hand. Even if not everything goes smoothly, there will be a solution. The overall trend is looking up, so keep that in mind, keep moving forward, and don't look back!

Money. Financially, June is not bad for you at all. You will have regular income, and significantly more of it. Expect the largest sums to come in on June 7, 8, 16, 17, 26, and 27.

Your expenses are low, and most of them are related to meetings at work, entertainment, or your loved ones.

Love and family. Virgos who are part of the working world might leave their personal lives on the back burner this month, work comes first! But if your personal life is the focus, get ready for some changes, not all of which are going to be positive.

If your relationship is literally hanging by a thread, remember that that thread can break at any time. That may be in June, or perhaps a little later. Severe Saturn has been in the sector of your sky responsible for marriage and long-term partnerships. Consider this a serious stress test for your relationship. Are you ready for it? Either way, there are things for you to think about. If you are facing difficulties with your spouse or partner, turn to friends, whose influence may smooth things over, but they are unlikely to solve this for you.

Health. In June, you are as vibrant as ever, and have no need to fear falling ill.

.

July

New York Time			London Time		
Calendar Day	Lunar Day	Lunar Day Start Time	Calendar Day	Lunar Day	Lunar Day Start Time
01/07/2023	15	6:54 PM	01/07/2023	14	7:30 PM
02/07/2023	16	7:58 PM	02/07/2023	15	8:37 PM
03/07/2023	17	8:55 PM	03/07/2023	16	9:33 PM
04/07/2023	18	9:44 PM	04/07/2023	17	10:16 PM
05/07/2023	19	10:25 PM	05/07/2023	18	10:49 PM
06/07/2023	20	11:00 PM	06/07/2023	19	11:15 PM
07/07/2023	21	11:31 PM	07/07/2023	20	11:38 PM
09/07/2023	22	12:01 AM	08/07/2023	21	11:58 PM
10/07/2023	23	12:29 AM	10/07/2023	22	12:18 AM
11/07/2023	24	12:59 AM	11/07/2023	23	12:39 AM
12/07/2023	25	1:32 AM	12/07/2023	24	1:02 AM
13/07/2023	26	2:08 AM	13/07/2023	25	1:30 AM
14/07/2023	27	2:49 AM	14/07/2023	26	2:04 AM
15/07/2023	28	3:36 AM	15/07/2023	27	2:46 AM
16/07/2023	29	4:28 AM	16/07/2023	28	3:36 AM
17/07/2023	30	5:24 AM	17/07/2023	29	4:34 AM
17/07/2023	1	2:33 PM	17/07/2023	1	7:33 PM
18/07/2023	2	6:22 AM	18/07/2023	2	5:37 AM
19/07/2023	3	7:21 AM	19/07/2023	3	6:43 AM
20/07/2023	4	8:20 AM	20/07/2023	4	7:50 AM
21/07/2023	5	9:19 AM	21/07/2023	5	8:56 AM
22/07/2023	6	10:17 AM	22/07/2023	6	10:03 AM
23/07/2023	7	11:15 AM	23/07/2023	7	11:09 AM
24/07/2023	8	12:15 PM	24/07/2023	8	12:17 PM
25/07/2023	9	1:16 PM	25/07/2023	9	1:27 PM
26/07/2023	10	2:20 PM	26/07/2023	10	2:39 PM
27/07/2023	11	3:26 PM	27/07/2023	11	3:53 PM
28/07/2023	12	4:33 PM	28/07/2023	12	5:07 PM
29/07/2023	13	5:39 PM	29/07/2023	13	6:16 PM
30/07/2023	14	6:39 PM	30/07/2023	14	7:17 PM
31/07/2023	15	7:32 PM	31/07/2023	15	8:07 PM

You can find the description of each lunar day in the chapter "A Guide to The Moon Cycle and Lunar Days"

This month, you will have to turn to others for support. They will be people you love and trust. You are turning a page on the past, but the future is blurry, and you can't go it alone!

Work. Virgos who are part of the working world will have to solve many difficult tasks this month. For business owners and managers, a partner will have become increasingly difficult to deal with, and during the last 10 days of July, that will be more noticeable than ever. You may experience open disagreements, which may turn into an outright conflict.

Those planning a trip or to open their business in another city or abroad may also face challenges this month, and most of them will appear during the first two weeks of July. In September, however, things will all be resolved, thanks to your hard work and perseverance.

In all areas, July is a good month for seeing old friends or people who are highly placed in society. Some of them may become valuable mediators in any conflict involving your partners.

Money. In July, you can expect money troubles, mainly due to a difficult situation at work or problems in your personal life. Remember that sooner or later, we all reveal the thorn in our side, and that may be a clue to how this plays out.

Love and family. Those who managed to avoid any problems at work will be in for an unpleasant surprise in their personal life.

Couples who are on the rocks have arrived at the point that their relationship is literally hanging by a thread. Any misstep, and that thread is sure to break. The last 10 days of the month will be the most difficult time for you, as anything you do may lead to an angry response from your partner. Remember that any conflict could be your last, and act accordingly. However, if the love is truly gone, you can ignore this advice.

Many couples will notice that their relationship needs a lot of tact, attention, and understanding. Keep that in mind if you have any desire to remain together. This applies whether you are married or not.

Health. During the first 20 days of July, you are feeling vibrant and have no reason to fear falling ill. During the last 10 days of the month, however, you may feel run-down after all of the challenges you have been facing, so plan for some time to relax and focus on yourself. This is especially the case for the elderly and those who suffer from chronic illnesses.

August

New York Time			London Time		
Calendar Day	Lunar Day	Lunar Day Start Time	Calendar Day	Lunar Day	Lunar Day Start Time
01/08/2023	16	8:17 PM	01/08/2023	16	8:45 PM
02/08/2023	17	8:56 PM	02/08/2023	17	9:15 PM
03/08/2023	18	9:30 PM	03/08/2023	18	9:40 PM
04/08/2023	19	10:01 PM	04/08/2023	19	10:02 PM
05/08/2023	20	10:31 PM	05/08/2023	20	10:22 PM
06/08/2023	21	11:01 PM	06/08/2023	21	10:44 PM
07/08/2023	22	11:33 PM	07/08/2023	22	11:07 PM
09/08/2023	23	12:09 AM	08/08/2023	23	11:33 PM
10/08/2023	24	12:49 AM	10/08/2023	24	12:05 AM
11/08/2023	25	1:34 AM	11/08/2023	25	12:44 AM
12/08/2023	26	2:24 AM	12/08/2023	26	1:32 AM
13/08/2023	27	3:18 AM	13/08/2023	27	2:27 AM
14/08/2023	28	4:16 AM	14/08/2023	28	3:29 AM
15/08/2023	29	5:14 AM	15/08/2023	29	4:34 AM
16/08/2023	1	5:38 AM	16/08/2023	30	5:41 AM
16/08/2023	2	6:13 AM	16/08/2023	1	10:38 AM
17/08/2023	3	7:12 AM	17/08/2023	2	6:47 AM
18/08/2023	4	8:10 AM	18/08/2023	3	7:54 AM
19/08/2023	5	9:09 AM	19/08/2023	4	9:00 AM
20/08/2023	6	10:08 AM	20/08/2023	5	10:07 AM
21/08/2023	7	11:08 AM	21/08/2023	6	11:16 AM
22/08/2023	8	12:10 PM	22/08/2023	7	12:25 PM
23/08/2023	9	1:13 PM	23/08/2023	8	1:37 PM
24/08/2023	10	2:18 PM	24/08/2023	9	2:49 PM
25/08/2023	11	3:22 PM	25/08/2023	10	3:59 PM
26/08/2023	12	4:23 PM	26/08/2023	11	5:02 PM
27/08/2023	13	5:18 PM	27/08/2023	12	5:56 PM
28/08/2023	14	6:06 PM	28/08/2023	13	6:38 PM
29/08/2023	15	6:48 PM	29/08/2023	14	7:12 PM
30/08/2023	16	7:24 PM	30/08/2023	15	7:39 PM
31/08/2023	17	7:57 PM	31/08/2023	16	8:03 PM

You can find the description of each lunar day in the chapter "A Guide to The Moon Cycle and Lunar Days"

This month, you will need to display both restraint and caution. August is not a particularly favorable time for you. Sometimes, we go through times like these, that is why the stars recommend that you ride it out rather than rushing into battle.

Work. This is not a good time for you at work. Those with connections to colleagues in other cities or abroad will face numerous challenges.

You may have to contend with the laws of another country, or legal hiccups on your road to success. A difficult relationship with a past partner may also come to a head. Conflict is likely all month long, but the second half will be particularly tense.

During this time, you might decide to react aggressively, but that will only exacerbate an already-difficult situation. Though delicate issues involving colleagues from faraway might be temporary, a challenging relationship with a colleague might become a longstanding, chronic issue. Keep that in mind and avoid beating your head against the wall – this time, it might turn out to be made of steel.

All month long, Venus will be in retrograde, and starting on August 23, Mercury will join it. These aspects mean that August is not a time for any permanent decision-making or hasty moves.

Make a point of being less active this month than usual, and watch your back, because you might also run into secret enemies and information that you'd rather keep quiet coming to the surface.

Money. With so many difficulties at work this month, you can expect money troubles to follow. However, On August 19-21, 28, and 29, you can count on receiving a decent sum.

Love and family. If your life path has taken you to a place where you are more focused on your personal life than work, here, you can expect to face some tough times. Your relationship with your spouse or partner might totally fall apart, and this will be partly your fault. Perhaps you will finally have to answer for mistakes made in the past.

The planets are aligned in such a way that even couples who get along might find themselves dealing with tensions.

Severe Saturn, which now rules your connections, suggests that by keeping a careful attitude toward one another, you will be able to avoid many problems.

Health. Those lucky enough to avoid unpleasant situations at home and at work may experience health issues in August. Be especially careful if you are elderly or suffer from chronic conditions. The stars recommend that you spend some time taking care of yourself and taking a step back from work. All month long, be careful driving and traveling. There is a rather high risk of road accidents this month.

September

New York Time			London Time		
Calendar Day	Lunar Day	Lunar Day Start Time	Calendar Day	Lunar Day	Lunar Day Start Time
01/09/2023	18	8:28 PM	01/09/2023	17	8:24 PM
02/09/2023	19	8:59 PM	02/09/2023	18	8:46 PM
03/09/2023	20	9:32 PM	03/09/2023	19	9:09 PM
04/09/2023	21	10:07 PM	04/09/2023	20	9:34 PM
05/09/2023	22	10:46 PM	05/09/2023	21	10:05 PM
06/09/2023	23	11:30 PM	06/09/2023	22	10:43 PM
08/09/2023	24	12:19 AM	07/09/2023	23	11:28 PM
09/09/2023	25	1:13 AM	09/09/2023	24	12:21 AM
10/09/2023	26	2:09 AM	10/09/2023	25	1:21 AM
11/09/2023	27	3:08 AM	11/09/2023	26	2:25 AM
12/09/2023	28	4:07 AM	12/09/2023	27	3:31 AM
13/09/2023	29	5:05 AM	13/09/2023	28	4:38 AM
14/09/2023	30	6:04 AM	14/09/2023	29	5:45 AM
14/09/2023	1	9:40 PM	15/09/2023	1	2:40 AM
15/09/2023	2	7:03 AM	15/09/2023	2	6:52 AM
16/09/2023	3	8:02 AM	16/09/2023	3	7:59 AM
17/09/2023	4	9:02 AM	17/09/2023	4	9:07 AM
18/09/2023	5	10:03 AM	18/09/2023	5	10:16 AM
19/09/2023	6	11:06 AM	19/09/2023	6	11:27 AM
20/09/2023	7	12:10 PM	20/09/2023	7	12:39 PM
21/09/2023	8	1:13 PM	21/09/2023	8	1:48 PM
22/09/2023	9	2:13 PM	22/09/2023	9	2:52 PM
23/09/2023	10	3:09 PM	23/09/2023	10	3:48 PM
24/09/2023	11	3:58 PM	24/09/2023	11	4:33 PM
25/09/2023	12	4:41 PM	25/09/2023	12	5:09 PM
26/09/2023	13	5:18 PM	26/09/2023	13	5:38 PM
27/09/2023	14	5:52 PM	27/09/2023	14	6:03 PM
28/09/2023	15	6:24 PM	28/09/2023	15	6:25 PM
29/09/2023	16	6:55 PM	29/09/2023	16	6:46 PM
30/09/2023	17	7:27 PM	30/09/2023	17	7:08 PM

You can find the description of each lunar day in the chapter "A Guide to The Moon Cycle and Lunar Days"

Expect September to be overall positive for you. Your promising future looks more tangible every day, and it has a lot of good things in store for you! All you have to do is cut ties with the past.

Work. You will likely be able to divide September into two very different periods. During the first two weeks of the month, your ruler, Mercury, will be in retrograde, so you will see a lot of ups and downs, not to mention doubt when it comes to some matters. Most likely, this will involve a difficult relationship with a former business partner.

To summarize, things are about to reach a breaking point, and it's still unclear what your role is in all of this. It seems that the time has come to cut your losses and move on. You are about to embark on a new future, with new business and new partners. You will make a decision during the second half of the month, and the stars predict that it will be the right one. If you still have some material issues to deal with, they will be resolved in your favor.

This month, you will reach your goals when it comes to any planned move, work, or opening your business in another city or abroad. Closer to the end of September, you might take a trip or make a move. The second half of the month is a good time to start any studies, new ideas, or overhaul your life.

Money. The second half of September is a good time for your finances, and you can expect the largest sums to come in on September 25-27.

Love and family. Things in your personal life are still going well. Couples on the rocks might decide to divorce, and most likely, your spouse will have the last word.

During the first half of the month, you might be hoping to leave everything as it is, but that is unlikely to happen. There are many fish in the sea, however, and there is someone out there for you.

Couples who get along will be making plans for the future and working to make them a reality. If you want to move to another city or abroad, the next three months are the best time to make that happen.

Health. In September, you are feeling sluggish, and that is most noticeable during the first two weeks of the month. The stars advise you to spend less time getting upset over things and remember that Rome wasn't built in a day. If you keep your cool, you will have a lot less problems.

October

New York Time			London Time		
Calendar Day	Lunar Day	Lunar Day Start Time	Calendar Day	Lunar Day	Lunar Day Start Time
01/10/2023	18	8:02 PM	01/10/2023	18	7:33 PM
02/10/2023	19	8:40 PM	02/10/2023	19	8:02 PM
03/10/2023	20	9:23 PM	03/10/2023	20	8:38 PM
04/10/2023	21	10:11 PM	04/10/2023	21	9:21 PM
05/10/2023	22	11:04 PM	05/10/2023	22	10:12 PM
07/10/2023	23	12:01 AM	06/10/2023	23	11:11 PM
08/10/2023	24	12:59 AM	08/10/2023	24	12:14 AM
09/10/2023	25	1:58 AM	09/10/2023	25	1:20 AM
10/10/2023	26	2:57 AM	10/10/2023	26	2:27 AM
11/10/2023	27	3:56 AM	11/10/2023	27	3:34 AM
12/10/2023	28	4:54 AM	12/10/2023	28	4:40 AM
13/10/2023	29	5:54 AM	13/10/2023	29	5:48 AM
14/10/2023	30	6:54 AM	14/10/2023	30	6:56 AM
14/10/2023	1	1:55 PM	14/10/2023	1	6:55 PM
15/10/2023	2	7:55 AM	15/10/2023	2	8:06 AM
16/10/2023	3	8:59 AM	16/10/2023	3	9:17 AM
17/10/2023	4	10:03 AM	17/10/2023	4	10:29 AM
18/10/2023	5	11:07 AM	18/10/2023	5	11:40 AM
19/10/2023	6	12:08 PM	19/10/2023	6	12:46 PM
20/10/2023	7	1:05 PM	20/10/2023	7	1:44 PM
21/10/2023	8	1:55 PM	21/10/2023	8	2:32 PM
22/10/2023	9	2:38 PM	22/10/2023	9	3:09 PM
23/10/2023	10	3:16 PM	23/10/2023	10	3:40 PM
24/10/2023	11	3:50 PM	24/10/2023	11	4:05 PM
25/10/2023	12	4:21 PM	25/10/2023	12	4:27 PM
26/10/2023	13	4:51 PM	26/10/2023	13	4:48 PM
27/10/2023	14	5:22 PM	27/10/2023	14	5:09 PM
28/10/2023	15	5:55 PM	28/10/2023	15	5:32 PM
29/10/2023	16	6:32 PM	29/10/2023	16	4:59 PM
30/10/2023	17	7:13 PM	30/10/2023	17	5:31 PM
31/10/2023	18	8:00 PM	31/10/2023	18	6:11 PM

You can find the description of each lunar day in the chapter "A Guide to The Moon Cycle and Lunar Days"

This month, you will have an excellent opportunity to fix something you dealt with in the recent past. It seems that life is slowly improving!

Work. Things are palpably better for you at work. Your relationships with colleagues in other cities or abroad are better, and you might be involved in meetings, negotiations, or business travel. Despite the positive trend, however, there are still some problems on the horizon. They may show up at the very end of October and continue into November.

Another issue may be your relationship with a business partner. You are highly aware of the crux of the issue, as you have been here before. It may be worth separating, and in that case, resolving your financial issues in relative peace.

Those looking for a new job or to study in another city or abroad might count on doing just that this month.

Money. Financially, October is not bad at all. You will have regular income, and significantly more of it than usual. Expect the largest sums to come in on October 3, 4, 13, 14, 22, and 23. Your expenses are mostly related to your personal life and the demands of your children and loved ones, but they will still be relatively low.

Love and family. Your personal life is seeing a continuation of things that began in the recent past. Couples who are feuding or divorcing might confirm their position. Your partner will still be harsh and unbending, and there will be no way to get through to him or her. You still have your children together, but they will be unable to fully resolve this for you. Naturally, this only applies to those who have been warring for some time.

Alternatively, your spouse or loved one will continue to face challenges and you will have to provide them with moral and financial support. The third possibility is that you may have to spend some time apart.

Those moving somewhere faraway might deal with a series of issues this month.

Unmarried couples will have an easier time in October, and their relationship will not suffer.

Your relationship with your relatives is more complicated during the last 10 days of October, and you may experience conflict, which will continue into November.

Health. In October, you are feeling vigorous and have no reason to fear falling ill. However, after October 20, the stars recommend that you be careful when driving or traveling.

November

New York Time			London Time		
Calendar Day	Lunar Day	Lunar Day Start Time	Calendar Day	Lunar Day	Lunar Day Start Time
01/11/2023	19	8:52 PM	01/11/2023	19	7:00 PM
02/11/2023	20	9:49 PM	02/11/2023	20	7:57 PM
03/11/2023	21	10:47 PM	03/11/2023	21	9:00 PM
04/11/2023	22	11:47 PM	04/11/2023	22	10:06 PM
05/11/2023	23	11:46 PM	05/11/2023	23	11:13 PM
07/11/2023	24	12:45 AM	07/11/2023	24	12:20 AM
08/11/2023	25	1:43 AM	08/11/2023	25	1:26 AM
09/11/2023	26	2:42 AM	09/11/2023	26	2:33 AM
10/11/2023	27	3:42 AM	10/11/2023	27	3:41 AM
11/11/2023	28	4:43 AM	11/11/2023	28	4:50 AM
12/11/2023	29	5:46 AM	12/11/2023	29	6:02 AM
13/11/2023	1	4:27 AM	13/11/2023	30	7:15 AM
13/11/2023	2	6:51 AM	13/11/2023	1	9:27 AM
14/11/2023	3	7:57 AM	14/11/2023	2	8:28 AM
15/11/2023	4	9:01 AM	15/11/2023	3	9:38 AM
16/11/2023	5	10:00 AM	16/11/2023	4	10:40 AM
17/11/2023	6	10:53 AM	17/11/2023	5	11:31 AM
18/11/2023	7	11:39 AM	18/11/2023	6	12:12 PM
19/11/2023	8	12:18 PM	19/11/2023	7	12:44 PM
20/11/2023	9	12:52 PM	20/11/2023	8	1:10 PM
21/11/2023	10	1:23 PM	21/11/2023	9	1:32 PM
22/11/2023	11	1:52 PM	22/11/2023	10	1:52 PM
23/11/2023	12	2:22 PM	23/11/2023	11	2:12 PM
24/11/2023	13	2:53 PM	24/11/2023	12	2:34 PM
25/11/2023	14	3:27 PM	25/11/2023	13	2:58 PM
26/11/2023	15	4:05 PM	26/11/2023	14	3:27 PM
27/11/2023	16	4:49 PM	27/11/2023	15	4:03 PM
28/11/2023	17	5:39 PM	28/11/2023	16	4:48 PM
29/11/2023	18	6:35 PM	29/11/2023	17	5:42 PM
30/11/2023	19	7:33 PM	30/11/2023	18	6:43 PM

You can find the description of each lunar day in the chapter "A Guide to The Moon Cycle and Lunar Days"

In order to leverage this month as best you can, you will need to be more precise as you react to the mood and initiative of those around you. Venus is on your side, which means that you will achieve a lot.

Work. This month, your interests are probably related to somewhere faraway. Not everything in this direction will go as you had planned, however. In mid-November, you will face unexpected obstacles, which may include the laws of another country, or possibly a difficult relationship with a colleague from afar.

Your relationships with former business partners, who caused you a lot of problems as 2023 draws to a close, has improved somewhat, but that does not mean that things are anywhere near resolved. Right now, though, you will have an opportunity to engage in peaceful negotiations and constructively work to fix things from the past.

This month will be action-packed, which is both good and bad. It will cause you a lot more work, but that's just life!

Money. After November 10, your financial situation will be looking up. Expect to receive the largest sums on November 1, 2,10, 11, 18-20, 27, and 28. Your expenses are low, and all of them are both predictable and reasonable.

Love and family. In your personal life, you will have to overcome difficult issues involving those around you. That is likely your relationships with close relatives. Someone in your family member has probably had a serious argument and you will need to help those close to you find common ground.

Those who are moving somewhere faraway will deal with various hurdles – the laws of another country, or various logistical challenges.

Most of these problems will occur during the middle of the month, but thanks to your efforts, they will eventually fade away.

Divorcing couples or those who are on the rocks will still have a difficult relationship, but things are likely to improve. Your children might help you achieve that, or perhaps your desire to smooth the rough edges will be motivation enough.

Your partner may be unwilling to meet you halfway, but there is reason to remember that if the mountain will not come to Mohammed, then Mohammed must go to the mountain, and act accordingly. You may be pleasantly surprised by the reaction.

Health. This month, you are energetic and active, but stressed and anxious. If that sounds like you, then remember that the best way to relax is by getting enough sleep. Be careful when driving and traveling – the second 10 days of the month will be the most dangerous time.

December

New York Time			London Time		
Calendar Day	Lunar Day	Lunar Day Start Time	Calendar Day	Lunar Day	Lunar Day Start Time
01/12/2023	20	8:33 PM	01/12/2023	19	7:49 PM
02/12/2023	21	9:34 PM	02/12/2023	20	8:57 PM
03/12/2023	22	10:33 PM	03/12/2023	21	10:04 PM
04/12/2023	23	11:31 PM	04/12/2023	22	11:11 PM
06/12/2023	24	12:29 AM	06/12/2023	23	12:17 AM
07/12/2023	25	1:28 AM	07/12/2023	24	1:24 AM
08/12/2023	26	2:28 AM	08/12/2023	25	2:32 AM
09/12/2023	27	3:30 AM	09/12/2023	26	3:42 AM
10/12/2023	28	4:34 AM	10/12/2023	27	4:54 AM
11/12/2023	29	5:40 AM	11/12/2023	28	6:08 AM
12/12/2023	30	6:46 AM	12/12/2023	29	7:21 AM
12/12/2023	1	6:32 PM	12/12/2023	1	11:32 PM
13/12/2023	2	7:49 AM	13/12/2023	2	8:28 AM
14/12/2023	3	8:46 AM	14/12/2023	3	9:25 AM
15/12/2023	4	9:36 AM	15/12/2023	4	10:11 AM
16/12/2023	5	10:18 AM	16/12/2023	5	10:47 AM
17/12/2023	6	10:55 AM	17/12/2023	6	11:15 AM
18/12/2023	7	11:27 AM	18/12/2023	7	11:38 AM
19/12/2023	8	11:56 AM	19/12/2023	8	11:59 AM
20/12/2023	9	12:25 PM	20/12/2023	9	12:19 PM
21/12/2023	10	12:55 PM	21/12/2023	10	12:39 PM
22/12/2023	11	1:27 PM	22/12/2023	11	1:02 PM
23/12/2023	12	2:02 PM	23/12/2023	12	1:28 PM
24/12/2023	13	2:43 PM	24/12/2023	13	2:00 PM
25/12/2023	14	3:30 PM	25/12/2023	14	2:41 PM
26/12/2023	15	4:23 PM	26/12/2023	15	3:30 PM
27/12/2023	16	5:20 PM	27/12/2023	16	4:28 PM
28/12/2023	17	6:20 PM	28/12/2023	17	5:33 PM
29/12/2023	18	7:21 PM	29/12/2023	18	6:40 PM
30/12/2023	19	8:21 PM	30/12/2023	19	7:48 PM
31/12/2023	20	9:20 PM	31/12/2023	20	8:56 PM

You can find the description of each lunar day in the chapter "A Guide to The Moon Cycle and Lunar Days"

This month, you will need to show flexibility and the ability to maneuver in order to steer things to the right track, whether at work or in love. You will manage to avoid confrontation if you do this and remember that bad peace is better than a good war.

Work. For anything work-related, December is a fairly difficult time. Once again, your relationship with colleagues from other cities or abroad is worsening, and you may experience hold ups and even open confrontation.

This is a temporary situation – as December draws to a close, your difficulties will fade away, though for now, you will have to work on it. Remember that this situation has been around for a while, and there is not much you can do about it. At least, for now. The ball is in your partners' court, and you will have to either acquiesce to their demands or find someone new to work with.

From December 13 to January 2, 2024, your ruler, Mercury, will be in retrograde, and that means that you may not behave as constructively as you can. The stars recommend wavering less and sleep on anything before making a big decision. Think about the future and not just the moment. You will be facing an important period as you move away from the past, but the future is not quite clear yet, which is sure to make things harder, but it is what it is.

Money. Financially, December is neutral for you. Your income is modest, but so are your expenses. Your main expenses will be your children, home, and loved ones.

Love and family. For many Virgos, the most important events of December will take place at home and within their families. Here, you are also seeing some major changes. That may be the continuation of preparations related to a move to another city or abroad, or alternatively, you are embarking on a separation or divorce, and starting a new life somewhere new.

The issue of a move will lead to a lot of challenges this month, possibly related to documents, the laws of other countries, or logistics – you will have to overcome one of these matters, which will be the backdrop of the entire month.

Divorcing couples are still connected by their children, but they won't be able to count on their influence being enough to fix things. Most likely, any red lines were crossed long ago and there is no way back.

Alternatively, your spouse will suffer a major illness or problems at work, which will make life difficult for the entire family.

Health. This month, you are feeling sluggish, but you have no reason to fear falling seriously ill as long as you lead a healthy lifestyle and get some exercise in the mornings.

Virgo Description

Sign. Feminine, earth, mutable.

Ruler. Mercury.

Exaltation. Mercury.

Temperament. Melancholic, restrained, cold yet anxious.

Positive traits. Hard-working, business-minded, intelligent and with a great memory, teachable, methodical, punctual, pragmatic, neat, dignified.

Negative traits. Formal, petty, thoughtless, anxious, indecisive, self-centered, self-interested, cunning, prone to flattery, resentful, capricious, greedy, vain.

Weaknesses in the body. Gastro-intestinal tract, solar plexus, pylorus, duodenum, cecum, pancreas, spleen, liver, gallbladder, autonomic nervous system, abdominal cavity.

Metal. Brass.

Minerals. For a talisman- yellow agate and jasper. Generally- yellow sapphire, amber, citrine, chrysolite.

Numbers. 5, 10.

Day. Wednesday.

Colors. Bright green and yellow brown.

Virgo energy

Virgo's personality is colored by the energy of two planets – Mercury and Proserpina. Mercury impacts Virgos differently than it does Geminis, creating a calmer, less independent character. One might say that Proserpina's unhurried effect "slows down" Mercury's influence in Virgo. Virgo and Gemini share a brilliant intellect, but Proserpina is a powerful planet that unleashes the swirl of time. She endows her children with a sense of duty, punctuality, clarity, analytical abilities, a tendency to study the root cause of any problem, grow, and transition to a higher state. In order to that to happen, though, the conscious must work, which is what Virgo has been doing her entire life. Virgo is an Earth sign, making her a practical materialist guided by logic and common sense.

Astrological portrait of Virgo

Virgo is a sign associated with work, service, and duty. It is a sign that is capable of overcoming difficulties. This is why Virgo is always concerned with her health and does not hesitate to seek medical attention. Virgos are willing to work tirelessly for a good cause. Their goals are clear and real rather than simply theoretical ideals. Virgos do not build pies in the sky, and their work is what gives life meaning. Virgos cannot tolerate laziness in others and will not aid those who refuse to work.

Virgos analyze. They are rational, with perfectly developed logic. They have a clear mind, with few illusions about life or other people. Even in love, they are capable of seeing their partner's shortcomings and turn to various methods to correct them. This does not mean that Virgos are devoid of emotions or purely driven by logic, however. Virgo's feelings are there, but she will only rarely reveal them. Even love is first and foremost a duty to Virgo. If someone is truly in need, she will happily step up and do whatever is necessary. Virgo is an intellectual sign, and people born under it constantly strive for new knowledge. They are skilled at absorbing information and memorizing facts. This is why many Virgos are known to their friends as a walking encyclopedia. They seem to know everything and give intelligent, practical advice on any topic. When asked about anything, it is as if they had a file in their head storing complete information on whatever topic is at hand, and they will not be satisfied until they have informed you of all of it. Virgo seeks knowledge to subdue matters with their mind – this is their great, cosmic task.

Virgos are thorough critics. But they are also extremely ambitious and painfully sensitive to any comments. If you start criticizing a Virgo, she will refute all of your arguments, and you will come to regret ever starting the discussion. Virgos are pedantic, judgmental, and calculated, and their ability to impose their opinion on others mean they are impervious to criticism.

Virgos may lack intuition and creativity. They have a need to touch and see everything with their own eyes, and it is difficult for them to grasp the abstract. They subject the entire world to excellent analysis but are less gifted at synthesizing what they perceive. This means that Virgos might have a tendency to miss the forest for the trees. Virgo's home is usually in perfect order. Less pleasant traits may be her coldness and emotional rigidity.

At her highest level, a Virgo is an erudite person full of information, but her greatest battle will be her own pedantry.

How to recognize a Virgo by appearance

A typical Virgo is a slender person with a somewhat disproportional figure. In adulthood, Virgo women may tend to lose more weight than they gain, and will stay in good physical shape, even in old age. Virgos have wide bones, and their facial expressions are serious and stern. They tend to be tall but are rarely excessively so. Their faces tend to be long, as is their nose, which thickens into the shape of a water droplet. Their features are thin and well-defined. They have small eyes. Virgos are modest and often shy, and do not seek to draw attention to themselves, even if they are famous.

Charting Virgo's Fate

In childhood and adolescence, Virgos will face great difficulties. Later, they will manage to reach stability and security. Virgo builds her own happiness through decades of hard work and trial and error. Virgos tend to suffer a crisis in their personal life between the ages of about 18 to 29. They may experience marriage followed by divorce. Perhaps it finding a suitable partner seems impossible. Virgos reach personal harmony rather late in life, after the age of 36, and in some cases, as late as 42.

A Guide to The Moon Cycle and Lunar Days

Since Ancient times, people have noticed that the moon has a strong influence on nature. Our Earth and everything living on it is a single living being, which is why the phases of the moon have such an effect on our health and mental state, and therefore, our lives. Remember Shakespeare and his description of Othello's jealousy in his famous tragedy:

"It is the very error of the moon, She comes more nearer Earth than she was wont And makes men mad."

If our inner rhythm is in harmony with that of the cosmos, we are able to achieve much more. People were aware of this a thousand years ago. The lunar calendar is ancient. We can find it among the ancient Sumerians (4000-3000 BC), the inhabitants of Mesopotamia, Native Americans, Hindus, and ancient Slavs. There is evidence that the Siberian Yakuts had a lunar calendar, as did the Malaysians.

Primitive tribes saw the moon as a source of fertility. Long before Christianity, the waxing moon was seen as favorable for planting new crops and starting a new business, for success and making money, while the waning moon was a sign that business would end.

What are the phases of the moon?

- Phase 1 – new moon
- Phase 2 – waxing crescent moon
- Phase 3 – first quarter moon
- Phase 4 – waxing gibbous moon
- Phase 5 – full moon
- Phase 6 – waning gibbous moon
- Phase 7 – third quarter moon
- Phase 8 – waning crescent moon

To simplify things, we can divide the month into two phases:
Waxing crescent moon - before the full moon
Waning crescent moon - after the full moon

New Moon

We cannot see the new moon, as it is hidden. People might complain about feeling weak, mental imbalance, and fatigue. During this time, we want to avoid taking on too much or overdoing things. Generally, people are not very responsive and react poorly to requests, which is why it is best to look out for yourself, while not keeping your plate too full.

The new moon is a bad time for advertising – it will go unnoticed. It is not worth preparing any presentations, parties, or loud gatherings. People are feeling constrained, not very social, and sluggish.

This is also a less than ideal time for surgery, as your recovery will be slow, and the likelihood of medical error is high.

It is also difficult to get an accurate diagnosis during the new moon – diseases might seem to be hidden, and doctors might not see the real underlying cause of what ails you.

The new moon is also a bad time for dates, and sexual encounters may be dissatisfying and leave you feeling disappointed. Ancient astrologers did not advise planning a wedding night during the new moon.

Waxing Crescent Moon

It is easy to identify a waxing crescent moon. If you draw an imaginary line between the two "horns", you should see the letter P. The waxing moon is then divided into one and two quarters.

During the first quarter moon, we need to focus on planning – setting goals and thinking of how we will set about achieving them. However, it is still a good idea to hold back a bit and not overdo things. Energy levels are still low, though they are growing along with the moon. It is still a good idea to avoid any medical procedures during this time.

The second quarter is a time for bold, decisive action. Things will come easy, and there is a greater chance of a lucky break. This is a good time for weddings, especially if the moon will be in Libra, Cancer, or Taurus. Nevertheless, it is a good idea to put off any advertising activities and public speaking until closer to the full moon, if you can.

Full Moon

During the full moon, the Earth is located between the sun and the moon. During this time, the moon is round and fully illuminated. This takes place during days 14-16 of the lunar cycle.

During the full moon, many people feel more vigorous than usual. They are emotional, sociable, and actively seeking more contact, so this may be a good time for any celebrations.

However, be careful not to drink too much – you can relax to the point that you lose control, and the consequences of that can be very unpleasant. If you are able to stick to moderation, there is no better time for a party!

The full moon is also the best time for advertising, as not only will your campaign be widely seen, people will be apt to remember it.

The full moon is also a favorable time for dates, and during this time, people are at their most open, romantic, and willing to tell each other something important that might take their relationship to the next level of trust and understanding.

Moreover, during the full moon, people feel a surge of energy, which may lead to hyperactivity, restlessness, and insomnia.

It will be harder to keep your emotions in check. You might face conflicts with friends, disasters, and accidents. During the full moon, any surgeries are **not a good idea**, as the risk of complications and bleeding is on the rise. Plastic surgery is also a bad idea, as swelling and bruises might be much worse than in another lunar phase. At the same time, the full moon is a good time to get an accurate diagnosis.

During this time, try to limit your calories and liquid intake (especially if you deal with bloating and excess weight), as your body is absorbing both calories and liquids faster during the full moon, and it can be very difficult to get rid of the weight later on.

Waning Crescent Moon

The full moon is over, and a new phase is beginning – the waning moon. This is a quieter time, when all of the jobs you started earlier are being partly or entirely completed (it all depends on the speed and scale).

Surgery will turn out much better if it is performed during the waning moon. Your recovery will be faster, and the likelihood of complications is much lower. If you have any plans to lose weight, the waning moon is the best time to do that. This is also a good time for quitting bad habits, such as smoking or cursing.

The waning moon can also be divided into the third and fourth quarters.

Third quarter - this is a favorable period, and you are able to resolve a lot of problems without conflict. People are calming down and ready to listen and take in information, while still being active. However, this is not the best time to begin any major projects, especially if you are unsure if you will be able to complete them by the start of the new lunar month.

The third quarter is a good time to get married, especially if the moon is in Cancer, Taurus, or Libra.

Fourth quarter – This is the most passive period of the lunar cycle. You are not as strong as usual. Your energy is lagging. You will be tired until reaching a new beginning. The best thing you can do as the lunar cycle comes to an end is to get things in order, and avoid anything that might get in your way at work or in personal relationships. Examine your successes and failures.

Now, let's discuss the lunar days in greater detail. For centuries, people around the world have described the influence of lunar days, and modern astrologers only add to this work, as they compare old texts to modern life.

The 1st lunar day

The first lunar day is extremely important for the rest of the lunar month. This is a much-needed day to carefully plan your activities and lay the groundwork for the rest of the lunar month. Remember that the first lunar day is not a good day for major activities, but rather for sitting down and planning things.

Avoid conflicts on this day, unless you want them to overshadow the rest of the month. Try to see the positive side of things and imagine that the lunar month will bring you good things both at work and in love. The more vividly you can imagine this, the sooner your desires will come to fruition. Perhaps it would be a good idea to jot down plans that will bring you closer to achieving your dreams. This is the best time for both manifesting and making wishes!

This is also a favorable day when it comes to seeking a new job or starting an academic program.

It is fine to go out on a date on the first lunar day, but limit any sexual contact, as your energy levels are low, and you are likely to end up disappointed.

Getting married on the first lunar day is not recommended.

Avoid getting a haircut – there are many indications that cutting your hair on the first lunar day will have a negative effect on your health and life expectancy.

Under no circumstances should you undergo any major cosmetic procedures, including plastic surgery. Energy levels are low, your skin is dull and almost stagnant. The results will not live up to your expectations, and in the worst-case scenario, you will end up looking worse than before. It is common for cosmetic procedures performed on this day to be disappointing or even useless. Even the best surgeons are less capable.

Your good dreams on the first lunar day foretell happiness and joy. Bad ones usually do not come true.

The 2ⁿᵈ lunar day

This is considered a lucky day, and is symbolized by a cornucopia. It is not an exaggeration to say that the second lunar day is a favorable time for both work and love. It is a time for action, and a great period to work on yourself, look for a new job, start something new, or complete any financial transaction, whether a sale or purchase. This is also a great time for creative and scientific insights, and a good time for any meeting – whether political or romantic.

Any romantic dates or sexual encounters during the second lunar day are unlikely to disappoint. This is also a good day for weddings or taking a trip with someone special.

During the second lunar day, the moon is beginning its waxing phase, which is a good time for anything you might to do nourish and restore your skin. This is a great time for any cosmetic procedures aimed at preservation, though it is best to put off any plastic surgery until the waning moon. If that is not possible, then the second lunar day is acceptable, if not ideal, and you will not run into any complications.

Folklore tells us that this is not a good day for a haircut, as that may lead to arguments with a loved one.

This is the best time for exercise – your body is in good shape, and you are able to handle new exercise regimens. If the moon happens to be in Scorpio, though, be careful.

This is a good day for anything positive, but avoid any conflicts, discussions about the status of your relationship, or litigation.

Dreams of the second lunar day are usually not prophetic.

The 3rd lunar day

On this day, we are usually able to make out a thin sliver of the lunar crescent. It is a longstanding tradition to show money during the new month – it is believed that as the moon grows, so will your savings.

However, astrological systems around the world consider this an unlucky, unfavorable day. It is not a good idea to travel, begin any new business, or give into your bad mood.

You might run into many a lot of problems at work on this day, which will cause you a lot of anxiety. However, it is a good day to take a step back and identify and set about fixing any flaws and shortcomings. Remember that everything tends to look worse on this day than it actually is.

It is not the time to ask management for anything – you are likely to walk away disappointed, and end up unfairly reprimanded rather than receiving a promotion or raise. Instead, focus on areas of work that need to be smoothed over or studied further. It will be clear what problems you are facing, and you will easily be able to find a remedy.

Do not rush to criticize your loved ones – things may not be as they appear. "Measure twice and cut once" is your motto on this day.

This is not a good day to get married, as the couple is likely to have a turbulent, short-lived marriage.

You can schedule a cosmetic procedure for this day, but only if it is relatively minor. Plastic surgery should wait.

Do exercises as usual, without overdoing it or adding any new routines.

Dreams on this day do not mean anything.

The 4ᵗʰ lunar day

These are relatively neutral days, in that they are unlikely to bring anything bad, but they also will not bring you any windfalls. The fourth lunar day is symbolized by a tree of paradise, the tree of knowledge, and the choice between good and evil. Things ultimately depend on us and our final decisions.

This is a great day for anything money-related – signing contracts, agreements, or even taking on credit. There are also a lot of contradictions on this day – on one hand, we are likely to receive money, which is a good thing, but on the other, we will have to give some of it away, which is never particularly fun or pleasant. There is good reason to consider all of your opportunities and possibilities before acting.

It is not a good day to get married, as the wedding will not be as fun as you had hoped. However, the fourth lunar day is, in fact, a good day for sex and conceiving a healthy child.

Be careful on this day if you happen to engage in any physical exercise, as it is not a good idea to overeat or abuse alcohol. Take care of yourself. Any illnesses which began on this day may be extremely dangerous, if they are not dealt with immediately.

Cosmetic procedures are not contraindicated, as long as they are to preserve your appearance. Plastic surgery can be performed if you truly feel it is necessary.

However, avoid getting a haircut, as it is unlikely to grow back healthily, and will become brittle and dull. However, if the moon is in Leo, you can disregard this advice.

Dreams may turn out to be real.

The 5th lunar day

Traditionally, the fifth lunar day is one of the worst of the lunar month. It is symbolized by a unicorn. Unicorns need to be tamed, but only a virgin is capable of doing so. Many people will feel drained on this day, or frustrated with themselves, those around them, and life in general.

Try to avoid arguments- any conflicts are likely to drag out for a long time, and then you may be overcome with guilt. This advice is relevant for both work and love.

Sexual encounters may be pleasant, but this is not a good day to plan a wedding, as it is likely to lead to a marriage full of unpleasant incidents.

Do not start any new businesses, or ask those around you for favors- you may be misunderstood and rejected.

It is fine to engage in physical exercise, but if you overdo it on this day, you may injure yourself.

Your energy levels are low. Cosmetic procedures may not be effective, and avoid any plastic surgeries.

It is good if you dream something connected with the road, trips or with movement in general. A bad dream might be a sign of a health problem which should be addressed.

The 6th lunar day

The symbol of the sixth lunar day is a cloud and a crane. This is a philosophical combination that suggests that it is not worth rushing things on these days. This is a very positive, lucky day for both work and love. Creative work will be especially successful, as will any attempts at opening a new business in your field.

The sixth lunar day is a good time for resolving any financial matters. There is one limitation, however – do not give anyone a loan, as they may not pay it back. But you can certainly sponsor and support those who are more vulnerable than you.

This day is a good time to go on a trip, whether close to home or far away.

This is also a good day for dates, weddings, and marriage proposals. Remember that energy is more romantic than sexual, so it is better to give the gift of roses and a bottle of champagne than hot, passionate sex.

It is a good idea to get some exercise, but do not overdo things, though you will probably not want to, either.

Cosmetic procedures will be successful, and you can even have plastic surgery performed, so long as the moon is not in Scorpio.

It is still a good idea to avoid getting your hair cut, as you might "cut off" something good in addition to your hair.

It is better to not discuss dreams as they are usually true. Your dreams of this day can remind you of something that needs to be completed as soon as possible.

The 7ᵗʰ lunar day

This is also a favorable lunar day, and it is symbolized by a fighting cock, which is an Avestan deity. Avoid any aggression on this day, and instead work on yourself, spend time at home or in nature. Avoid discussing the status of your relationship with anyone, arguing, or wishing bad things on anyone. Everything will come back to haunt you, remember, silence is golden.

Business negotiations and contracts will be successful. You can find support, sponsors, and people ready to help you in both words and deeds.

Lighten up with your colleagues and subordinates. Pay attention not only to their shortcomings, but also to their skills. This is a good day for reconciliation and creating both political and romantic unions.

The seventh lunar day is good for traveling, no matter how near or far from home.

It is also a favorable time for love and marriage.

Exercise moderately, and any plastic surgeries will go very smoothly, as long as the moon is not in Scorpio.

Dreams of this day may become a reality.

The 8ᵗʰ lunar day

The symbol for this day is a Phoenix, which symbolizes eternal rebirth and renewal, because this day is a great time for changes in all areas of your life. Your energy is likely to be high, and you want to do something new and unusual. This is a good time to look for a new job or begin studying something. Any out-of-the-box thinking is welcome, along with shaking things up a bit in order to improve your life.

However, avoid any financial transactions, as you may incur losses.

Avoid aggression. You can share your opinion by presenting well-founded arguments and facts, instead.

The phoenix rises from the ashes, so this is a good time to be careful with electrical appliances and fire in general. The risk of housefires is high.

Avoid any major financial transactions on the eighth day, as you may end up facing a series of complications. You can pay people their salaries, as this is unlikely to be a large sum.

This is a good day for weddings, but only if you and your future spouse are restless, creative souls and hope to achieve personal development through your marriage.

Any cosmetic procedures and plastic surgeries will go well today, as they are related to rebirth and renewal. Surgeons may find that they are true artists on this day!

You can try to change your hairstyle and get a fashionable haircut on this day.

You can trust your dreams seen on this day.

The 9th lunar day

The ninth lunar day is not particularly auspicious, and is even referred to as "Satan's" day. You may be overcome with doubt, suspicions, even depression and conflicts.

Your self-esteem will suffer, so don't overdo things physically, and avoid overeating or abusing alcohol.

This is a negative day for any business deals, travel, or financial transactions.

This is a particularly bad day for any events, so keep your head down at work and avoid any new initiatives.

It is better to avoid getting married on "Satan's" day, as the marriage will not last very long. Avoid sex, as well, but you can take care of your partner, listen them, and support them however they need.

Any cosmetic procedures will not have a lasting effect, and avoid any plastic surgery. A haircut will not turn out as you hoped.

Dreams of this day are usually prophetic.

The 10th lunar day

This is one of the luckiest days of the lunar month. It is symbolized by a spring, mushroom, or phallus. This is a time for starting a new business, learning new things, and creating.

The 10th lunar day is particularly lucky for business. Networking and financial transactions will be a success and bring hope. This is an ideal time for changing jobs, shifting your business tactics, and other renewals.

This is a perfect time for people in creative fields and those working in science, who may come up with incredible ideas that will bring many successful returns.

This is a very successful day for building a family and proposing marriage. This is a good time for celebrations and communication, so plan parties, meet with friends, and plan a romantic date.

One of the symbols for this day is a phallus, so sexual encounters are likely to be particularly satisfying.

The 10th lunar day is the best time to begin repairs, buying furniture, and items for home improvement.

You can exercise vigorously, and cosmetic procedures and plastic surgery will be very effective.

Dreams of this day will not come true.

The 11th lunar day

This is one of the best lunar days, and seen as the pinnacle of the lunar cycle. People are likely to be energetic, enthusiastic, and ready to move forward toward their goals.

The 11th lunar day is very successful for any financial transactions or business deals and meetings.

You might actively make yourself known, approach management to discuss a promotion, or look for a new job. This is an auspicious time for advertising campaigns, performances, and holding meetings.

Any trips planned will be a great success, whether near or far from home.

Romantic relationships are improving, sex is harmonious, and very desired.

Weddings held on this day will be fun, and the marriage will be a source of joy and happiness.

Exercise is a great idea, and you might even beat your own personal record.

This is an ideal time for any cosmetic procedures, but any more serious plastic surgeries might lead to a lot of bruising and swelling.

A haircut will turn out as you had hoped, and you can experiment a bit with your appearance.

You can ignore dreams of this day – usually they do not mean anything.

The 12th lunar day

This day is symbolized by the Grail and a heart. As we move closer to the full moon, our emotions are at their most open. During this time, if you ask someone for something, your request will be heeded. This is a day of faith, goodness, and divine revelations.

For business and financial transactions, this is not the most promising day. However, if you help others on this day, your good deeds are sure to come back to you.

This is a day for reconciliation, so do not try to explain your relationships, as no one is at fault, and it is better to focus on yourself, anyway.

Avoid weddings and sex on this day, but if you want to do what your partner asks, there is no better time.

Many may feel less than confident and cheerful during this day, so take it easy when working out. Avoid overeating, stay hydrated, and avoid alcohol.

The 12th lunar day is not the best for getting married or having sex, but the stars would welcome affection and a kind word.

Avoid getting a haircut, or any plastic surgeries. This is a neutral day for minor cosmetic procedures.

Nearly all dreams will come true.

The 13th lunar day

This day is symbolized by Samsara, the wheel of fate, which is very erratic and capable of moving in any direction. This is why the 13th lunar day is full of contradictions. In Indian traditions, this day is compared to a snake eating its own tail. This is a day for paying off old debts and returning to unfinished business.

Avoid beginning any new business on this day. It is preferable to finish old tasks and proofread your work. Information you receive on this day may not be reliable and must be verified.

It is worth resolving financial problems very carefully, and avoid arguments and conflict.

Do not change jobs on this day or go to a new place for the first time. Do not sit at home alone, though, go see old friends, parents, or older family members.

Minor cosmetic procedures are welcome on this day, but avoid any plastic surgery, as you may experience major swelling and bruising. Avoid any haircuts, too.

As a rule, all dreams will come true.

The 14th lunar day

It's a full moon! The 14th lunar day is one of the happiest, and it is symbolized by the trumpet. Pay attention – you may run into new, much-needed information. Networking will be successful, and you can confidently sign agreements, meet with people, and attend fun gatherings or other leisure activities. This is one of the best days for advertising, performances, and concerts, and those working in creative professions should keep this in mind, as should those who work in politics. Do not sit in place on this day – you need to get out and see others, make new connections, and try to be visible.

This is one of the best days for communication with and making requests from management, as your initiatives will be noticed and welcome. You might talk about a promotion, raise, or something similarly related to professional growth.

Couples will see their relationship is moving along well on this day, and it is also a good day for getting married.

Any sex on this day will be vigorous and memorable for a long time. The full moon is the best time for conceiving a child.

Any cosmetic procedures will be effective, but avoid any major changes to your appearance, as there is a high likelihood of bleeding and bruising. A haircut will turn out well.

Your dreams of this day will be more or less doubtful.

The 15th lunar day

It's a full moon! This day is symbolized by a serpent of fire. This is the energy peak of the entire lunar cycle, and a lot will depend on where you are focusing your energy.

You might face a lot of temptations on this day, for example, you might tell someone else's secret or your own to others, and come to regret it for a long time. The stars suggest exercising restraint in both your words and actions, as the 15th day of the lunar cycle is a day of deception and weaknesses.

This is a very active time, and many people might take unnecessary risks. This is not the best day for signing any agreements or contracts. For any performances, concerts, or advertising, however, this is one of the best days of the month.

You can get married on the 15th day, but only if you know each other well and have carefully considered your partnership, without any hasty decisions. This is also a favorable day for a second marriage.

Your romantic relationship is looking wonderful – you are on cloud 9, writing poetry, and deeply convinced of how right your partner is for you – and they feel the same way. It is important that this does not suddenly lead to an abrupt disappointment.

Avoid getting any haircuts on the 15th day of the month, as you may end up with a headache.

Conservative cosmetic procedures and creams will be very effective, but avoid any injections or plastic surgery today. Bleeding, swelling, and bruising are all but guaranteed.

Dreams on the 15th day nearly always come true.

The 16th lunar day

This day is symbolized by a dove. The full moon is over, and the moon is now in its waning phase. Usually, after the turbulent days of the full moon, people feel a bit under the weather. They are not cheerful, and want to avoid excess worry and give themselves a chance to breathe.

Don't ignore your body's wishes, take it easy with physical activities, and take some time for yourself. You might spend time in nature, in the forest, or at a country home.

The 16th day of the lunar month is a time for moderation in all areas – your behavior, eating, and even in your clothes. If you overate during the full moon period, now is the time to diet a bit or at least avoid fatty foods and meat.

This is not a promising day for resolving any financial matters. Keep your documents in order and get ready for any future meetings, instead. If you help a loved one, your good deed will come back 100 times over.

Avoid getting married today, as well as sex.

Cosmetic procedures are likely to be a success, especially if they are related to cleansing your skin, but it is best to avoid any plastic surgery or injections. Your body is not ready to accept them. A haircut will turn out as you hoped.

Any dreams are likely to come true, but that also depends on a correct interpretation.

The 17th lunar day

This day is represented by a vine and bell. It is a happy day and both successful and fun-filled. It is also a good time for negotiations, concluding small business deals, shaking up staffing, and creativity. However, you should keep in mind that the 17th day is only favorable for minor business, and you should avoid starting any major events.

Avoid any major financial transactions on this day. Do not give anyone money as a loan or borrow anything yourself, either.

Any travel, whether for business or pleasure, is likely to be a success.

The 17th day is a great time to get married, and an ideal day for dates. Any sexual encounters will bring you happiness and joy.

Avoid getting your hair cut on this day, but cosmetic procedures and plastic surgery will be a success. Women will look better than usual.

Your dreams are likely to come true in three days.

The 18th lunar day

This day is represented by a mirror. It is a difficult, and generally unpromising day, too. Just as the mirror reflects our imperfections back to us, we need to remember that moderation and modesty are key.

The 18th day is not a favorable time for any business meetings or financial transactions. You can, however work on jobs you already began. It is, however, a positive day for those who work in research or the creative fields.

Your motto of the day is to keep a cool head when it comes to your opportunities and the opportunities of those around you. This is relevant for both work and romantic relationships. It is not a good time to criticize others – any conflicts or arguments may lead to lasting consequences, which you do not need.

Avoid getting married on this day, as well as sexual encounters, which are likely to be disappointing. It is a good time to take a trip together, which will only be good for your relationship.

Avoid getting your hair cut, though this is a relatively neutral day for a haircut, which might turn out well, and though it will not exceed your expectations, it will also not leave you upset. Avoid any plastic surgeries.

Dreams on this day will come true.

The 19ᵗʰ lunar day

This is a very difficult day and it is represented by a spider. The energy is complicated, if not outright dangerous. Don't panic or get depressed, though – this is a test of your strength, and if you are able to hold onto all you have achieved. This is relevant for both work and love. On the 19ᵗʰ day, you should avoid taking any trips.

The energy of the 19ᵗʰ lunar day is very unfavorable for beginning any major projects, and business in general. Work on what you started earlier, get your affairs in order, think over your ideas and emotions, and check to make sure that everything you have done hitherto is living up to your expectations. Do not carry out any financial transactions or take out any loans – do not loan anyone else money, either. Do not ask your managers for anything as they are unlikely to listen to what you have to say, and make judgments instead.

This is a day when you might face outright deception, so do not take any risks and ignore rumors. Do not work on anything related to real estate or legal matters.

This is a very hard time for people with an unbalanced psyche, as they may experience sudden exacerbations or even suicidal ideations.

This is a very unlucky day to get married. Sexual encounters might be disappointing and significantly worsen your relationship.

Avoid any haircuts or cosmetic procedures or surgeries.

Your dreams of this day will come true.

The 20th lunar day

This is also a difficult day, though less so than the 19th. It is represented by an eagle. This is a good time to work on your own development and spiritual growth, by speaking to a psychologist or astrologer.

Avoid pride, anger, arrogance, and envy.

The 20th lunar day is a good time for people who are active and decisive. They will be able to easily overcome any obstacles, flying over them just like an eagle. If you have to overcome your own fears, you will be able to do so – don't limit yourself, and you will see that there is nothing to be afraid of. It is a good day for any financial transactions, signing contracts, and reaching agreements, as well as networking.

The 20th lunar day is a favorable time for those who work in the creative fields, as they will be able to dream up the idea that will open up a whole host of new possibilities. Avoid conflicts – they may ruin your relationship with a lot of people, and it will not be easy to come back from that.

This is a lucky day for getting married, but only if you have been with your partner for several years, now. Sexual encounters will not be particularly joyful, but they also will not cause you any problems.

Avoid getting your hair cut, but you can certainly get it styled. The 20th lunar day is a good day for those who are looking to lose weight. You will be able to do so quickly, and it will be easy for you to follow a diet.

Cosmetic procedures will be a success, as will any plastic surgeries.

Pay attention to dreams of this day as they are likely to come true.

The 21st lunar day

This is one of the most successful days of the lunar month, and it is symbolized by a herd of horses – imagine energy, strength, speed, and bravery. Everything you think up will happen quickly, and you will be able to easily overcome obstacles. A mare is not only brave but also an honest animal, so you will only experience this luck if you remember that honesty is always the best policy.

This is also a favorable day for business. Reaching new agreements and signing contracts, or dealing with foreign partners – it is all likely to be a success. Any financial issues will be resolved successfully.

Those in the creative world will be able to show off their talent and be recognized for their work. Anyone involved in the performing arts can expect success, luck, and recognition. A galloping herd of horses moves quickly, so you might transition to a new job, move to a new apartment, or go on a business trip or travel with your better half.

The 21st lunar day is one of the best to get married or have a sexual encounter.

This is a great time for athletes, hunters, and anyone who likes adventurous activities.

But for criminals and thieves, this is not a lucky or happy day – they will quickly be brought to justice.

Any haircuts or cosmetic procedures are likely to be a huge success and bring both beauty and happiness. You will recover quickly after any surgeries, perhaps without any swelling or bruising at all.

Dreams tend to not be reliable.

The 22nd lunar day

This day will be strange and contradictory. It is symbolized by the elephant Ganesha. According to Indian mythology, Ganesha is the patron saint of hidden knowledge. so this is a favorable day for anyone who is trying to learn more about the world and ready to find the truth, though this is often seen as a hopeless endeavor. This is a day for philosophers and wisemen and women. However, it is an inauspicious day for business, and unlikely to lead to resolving financial issues, signing contracts, agreements, or beginning new projects. You can expect trouble at work.

For creative people, and new employees, this is a successful day.

This is a good day for apologies and reconciliation.

Avoid getting married, though you can feel free to engage in sexual encounters.

For haircuts and cosmetic procedures, this is a fantastic day. Surgeries will also turn out, as long as the moon is not in Scorpio.

Dreams will come true.

The 23rd lunar day

This is a challenging day represented by a crocodile, which is a very aggressive animal. This is a day of strong energy, but it is also adventurous and tough. Your main task is to focus your energy in the right direction. There may be accidents, arguments, conflicts, fights, and violence, which is why it is important to strive for balance and calm.

Keep a close eye on your surroundings – there may be traitors or people who do not wish you well, so be careful.

However, this is still a favorable day for business – many problems will be resolved successfully. You are able to sign contracts and receive credit successfully, as long as you remain active and decisive in what you do.

This is not a day for changing jobs or working on real estate transactions or legal proceedings. This is not a favorable day for traveling, no matter how near or far you plan on going.

This is not a promising day to get married – things may end in conflict, if not an all-out brawl.

Sexual relations are not off the table, as long as the couple trusts one another.

Haircuts or cosmetic procedures will not turn out as you had hoped, so avoid them.

Dreams during this lunar day usually mean something opposite of what awaits you, so you can disregard them.

The 24th lunar day

This is a neutral, calm day that is symbolized by a bear. It is favorable for forgiveness and reconciliation.

This is also a good day for learning new things, reading, self-development, and taking time to relax in nature.

This is a great day for any type of financial activity, conferences, academic meetings, and faraway travel.

The 24th lunar day is a good time for love and getting married, as any marriage will be strong and lasting.

Cosmetic procedures and plastic surgery will be a success, and you can expect a speedy recovery.

Avoid getting a haircut on this day, however, as your hair will likely thin and grow back slowly.

Dreams of this lunar day are usually connected with your personal life.

The 25th lunar day

This is still another quiet day, symbolized by a turtle.

Just like a turtle, this is not a day to rush, and it is best to sit down and take stock of your life. This is a good time for resolving any personal problems, as the moon's energy makes it possible for you to calm down and find the right path.

This is also not a bad day for business. It is believed that any business you begin on this day is sure to be a success. This is especially the case for trade and any monetary activities.

The 25th lunar day is not a good day to get married, especially if the couple is very young.

This is a neutral day for sexual encounters, as the moon is waning, energy is low, so the decision is yours.

Avoid any cosmetic procedures, except those for cleansing your skin. This is not a favorable day for haircuts or plastic surgery – unless the moon is in Libra or Leo.

You can have a prophetic dream on this day.

The 26th lunar day

The 26th lunar day is full of contradictions and complicated. It is represented by a toad.

It is not time to start or take on something new, as nothing good will come of it. Avoid any major purchases, as you will later come to see that your money was wasted. The best thing you can do on this day is stay at home and watch a good movie or read a good book.

Avoid traveling on this day, as it may not turn out well.

The 26th lunar day is a negative day for any business negotiations and starting new businesses. Do not complete any business deals or financial transactions. Your colleagues may be arguing, and your managers may be dissatisfied. But if you have decided to leave your job, there is no better time to do so.

This is not a good day to get married, as both partners' expectations may fall flat, and they will soon be disappointed.

The waning moon carries a negative charge, so avoid any haircuts and surgeries, though you can get cosmetic procedures if they are relatively minor.

Your dreams will come true.

The 27th lunar day

The 27th lunar day is one of the best days of the month, and it is represented by a ship. You can boldly start any new business, which is sure to be promising. This is a great day for students, teachers, and learning new things. Any information that comes to you on this day may be extremely valuable and useful to you.

The 27th day is good for communication and travel, whether near or far from home, and no matter whether it is for work or pleasure.

This is also a good day for any professional activities or financial transactions. If there are people around you who need help, you must support them, as your good deeds will come back 100-fold.

Romantic dates will go well, though any weddings should be quiet and subdued. This is a particularly good day for older couples or second marriages.

The waning moon means that hair will grow back very slowly, but in general, you can expect a haircut to turn out well. This is a great day for plastic surgery or cosmetic procedures, as the results will be pleasing, and you will have a speedy recovery, without any bruising or swelling, most of the time.

However, beware if the moon is in Scorpio on this day – that is not a good omen for any plastic surgery.

Do not pay any attention to dreams on this day.

The 28th lunar day

This is another favorable day in the waning moon cycle, and it is represented by a lotus. This is a day of wisdom and spiritual awakening. If possible, spend part of the day in nature. It is important to take stock of the last month and decide what you need to do during its two remaining days.

This is a good time for any career development, changing jobs, conducting business, decision-making, and signing agreements, as well as going on a trip. You might conclude any business deal, hold negotiations, work with money and securities.

This is also a good day for any repairs or improvements around your home or apartment.

Any weddings today should be subdued and modest, and restricted to family members only. A loud, raucous wedding might not turn out very well.

Your hair will grow slowly, but any haircuts will turn out very elegant and stylish. Cosmetic procedures and surgeries are not contraindicated. You will recover quickly with little bruising and swelling.

Do not take any dreams too seriously.

The 29th lunar day

This is one of the most difficult days of the lunar month, and it is considered a Satanic day, unlucky for everyone and everything. It is symbolized by an octopus.

This is a dark day, and many will feel melancholy, depression, and a desire to simply be left alone. This is a day full of conflict and injuries, so be careful everywhere and with everyone. If you can, avoid any travel, and be particularly careful when handling any sharp objects. Do not engage in any business negotiations, sign any contracts, or take part in any networking.

Astrologers believe that anything you start on this day will completely fall apart. For once and for all, get rid of things that are impeding you from living your life. This is a good time to avoid people who you do find unpleasant.

This is also a time for fasting and limitations for everyone. Do not hold any celebrations, weddings, or have sexual relations – these events may not turn out as you hoped, and instead bring you nothing but suffering and strife.

Avoid getting a haircut, as well, as it will not make you look more beautiful and your hair will come back lifeless and dull. Cosmetic procedures can go ahead, but avoid any surgeries.

Dreams are likely to be true.

The 30ᵗʰ lunar day

There is not always a 30ᵗʰ lunar day, as some lunar months have only 29 days. This day is represented by a swan. The 30ᵗʰ lunar day is usually very short, and sometimes, it lasts less than an hour. This is a time for forgiveness and calm.

You might take stock of the last month, while also avoiding anything you do not need around you. Pay back loans, make donations, reconcile with those who recently offended you, and stop speaking to people who cause you suffering.

This is a good time for tying up loose ends, and many astrologers believe that it is also a good day to start new business.

However, avoid celebrations or weddings on this day. Spouses will either not live long, or they will quickly grow apart.

Do not get a haircut on this day, though cosmetic procedures are possible, as long as you avoid any surgeries.

Dreams promise happiness and should come true.